She

She

Creative Journey to Self-discovery
for Women of All Ages

Amy Rowling

Enjoy the Journey!

Word Studio
Tucson, Arizona
Falmouth, Massachusetts

2006

For information, permission, or questions concerning this book, please contact the publisher:

Word Studio
4072 E. 22nd Street #225
Tucson, AZ 85711
Or
P.O. Box 1104
N. Falmouth, MA 02556
www.word-studio.com

ISBN13: 978-0-9654360-5-2
ISBN10: 0-9654360-5-5

Published by

Word Studio

Printed in the United States of America
First Edition, 2006

Cover Design by Alicja Mann & Sebastian Lauber
Cover Photos by Amy Rowling

In memory of my father, Bill Rowling

This book is dedicated to my supportive family, my funny, wise, honest, and beautiful friends, the women of Cape Cod who appear in the images, and my dog Bandit, the truest of companions.

Editing
Alicja Mann

Copy Editing
George Shriver

Photography
Amy Rowling

Cover Design
Alicja Mann
Sebastian Lauber

Interior Design
Alicja Mann
Amy Rowling

Electronic Layout
Sebastian Lauber

Contents

Acknowledgments

Special thanks to my publisher, Alicja Mann, for taking this project under her wing with her characteristic creativity, intelligence, and energy.

To Robin Paris for recognizing the potential for a book in my poems and photographs.

To my sisters, Lynn Anderson and Sue Rowling, and my mother, Beverly Rowling, for their encouragement and support.

Introduction

I wrote these poems over a two-year period of spiritual and emotional growth before and after the death of my father in March 2003. Each of them is a marker for a particular stage in that growth.

Soon after my father's death I began photographing the faces, gestures, and expressions of local women and found that the images and poems influenced and enhanced one another. As the book took shape and women shared how they identified with the themes and emotions expressed in the writing and imagery, what began as a personal exploration became a springboard for healing others. With this in mind, I created a journaling space after each poem, with questions to encourage reflection, writing, and discussion. My hope for the book is that it will serve as a supportive and creative inspiration for women of all ages, individually or in groups.

The women who appear in this book are acquaintances or close friends of mine who were gracious and supportive enough to allow me the wonderful opportunity of photographing their faces at close range, to capture subtle and revealing characteristics of their personalities. These images, along with the intimacy of the poems, have the potential to comfort and inspire.

–Amy Rowling

Look within
Listen to your heart
Touch your truth
Taste the possibilities
Breathe in the courage

She

She

Sometimes the she
Isn't me
She's somebody
She's somebody
She lives and breathes
In you
In us
And me

I find her
In conversations
In the coffee shop
And the store
On the telephone
Walking in the woods
Along the shore

She's young, she's old
Porcelain, creamy
Weathered and worn

She's a grandmother
A child
She's outrageous
And a bore

She's sensual
And cold
Confident and shy

She's buxom
And wiry
Funny and dry

She's energetic
And weary
Self-reliant
And needy

She's proud
And humble
Generous and greedy

She's every longing
Laugh and tear
Revealed
I listen for her
Everywhere

She's my friend
She helps me heal

She

"She"

Do you feel connected to other women? Why or why not? Consider each descriptive stanza and how it relates to you and other women you know.

She   5

Within One Frame

She cannot bear
The ordinary
And yet it is what
She craves

Two caught
Within one frame
She longs to go
She longs to stay

To meld these
Women within
The restless
And peaceful
The mother
And child

A beautiful dance
These opposites
Could share

These two
Could remain
One body
Without judgment
Without shame

She

WRITING EXERCISE

"Within One Frame"

This poem describes a woman torn between two or more lives or dreams. Do you share these feelings? If so, when do they come up? How do you make important choices? Take a moment to reflect upon your values and goals.

She

Tug of Want

Longing for childhood
Revealed
Her dream of
Little girls playing on a hill

So far away
She runs
Toward them
Moving forward
To her past

She reaches them
They look at her
What is she doing?
Where has she gone?

They beckon her
To come and play
Her body stands
Immobile
Frozen with regret
Aware of time
Misplaced or wasted
Of her own potential
Not yet met

The youth and innocence
Of their faces
Bring tears
Of joy and tenderness
She relents
Grasps their hands

She lets them pull her
Right to left
A tug of war and want
Their persistence makes her laugh
She pulls them toward her finally
They walk and run and dance

She

WRITING EXERCISE

"Tug of Want"

Could you identify with this woman's feelings of running out of time? Do you worry about not reaching your goals? What can you do to work toward meeting your full potential today and in the near future? Make a list of your gifts, areas where you feel you have the most to offer. Create a goals list. Consider a goal gathering with friends. Bring your goals list and share with others. Reading your goals out loud can be a great motivator.

She

For the First Time

Deserving
Of love
Of health
Of wealth
She has not
Thought herself so

Although others
Have observed her
From the outside
And have believed
In her worth

The emptiness
She carries within
Absorbs possibilities
Soaks up the potential
Leaving her dry and barren

She waits
For others
To fill her well
To remind her
Of who she is
She cannot remember
Some days

The pain
Of this pattern
Has turned her
Eyes inward

She sees
Her heart
Great tenderness
The expanse
Of her gifts

For the first time
Repressed potential
Finding freedom
She now believes
In her own deserving

She

WRITING EXERCISE

"For the First Time"

Can you identify with feeling deserving or undeserving? What incidents or situations in your life trigger feelings of insecurity (lowered self-esteem) or empowerment?

She

Her Heart

Her heart
A ball of hardened tenderness
Packed tightly
No chance for release
Its beats
Weak and thready

A cold wall of protection
Surrounds her
Seems impermeable

He believes it can be broken
Picks at it like ice
Breaking it down
Piece
By
Piece

It keeps replenishing
He picks more fiercely

He is exhausted
His attempts are futile
His force of will and body
No match for her wall

Gentle light
Empathetic patience
The only way to reach her

Cradle her heart
In love and understanding
Here she can feel the warmth
The melting of wounds

It is the only way

She

Heart's Song

Child's frantic dancing
Inside her chest
Running and resting
Beats pound and thread

Hold
And listen
It wants to be heard
Feel its strength
As it finds
Its rhythm
In her

Ball of beats
Rhythmic and determined
Life
Skipping and dancing
Pushing forth

So tender
And strong
The source
Holding on
To life

Tenacious and fragile
Wounded and full
It thumps to be noticed
Acknowledged
And held

She tells it in rhythms
"I am here"
"You are loved"
"I am here"
"You are loved"

"Her Heart"

Do you identify with the woman, the man, or both people while reading this poem? Do you have emotional walls? Do you lack intimacy in relationships? Make a list of your fears in relationships. Make a list of the best methods to reach you. Share them with the significant other(s) in your life.

"Heart's Song"

Place your hands over your heart; pay attention to your breathing and the rhythm of your heart. Are the beats solid and consistent or are they quick and out of rhythm? Try this exercise when at rest and during times of stress. Use it as a method to ground you and connect you with your intuition.

She

Bag of Truth

She finds herself
In words
Her bag of truth
She calls it

Like Mary Poppins'
Bag of magic
Hers holds the phrases
Pages of her thoughts

The bag grows heavy
Her heart lightens
Pages
Add up

This impulse to write
Not so common
In the past
Reaches
A fevered pitch

Death and loss
Have taught her much
Although she still
Cannot express

Its impact
Has opened up
Some crevice
In her mind

The thoughts
Whirl round
If she's lucky
She'll find the pen
In time

To bring the words
To page
To bring her soul
To light

Reading back upon
Her truth
Validates
She is alive

She 25

WRITING EXERCISE

"Bag of Truth"

If you haven't begun journaling, try it! A helpful hint: have a small spiral journal or notebook that will fit inside your bag or purse. This allows you to write wherever you are. Waiting for people or appointments is not as irritating when you have writing materials available to you.

She

Worth

Money is paper
It balls up in her purse
In her pockets
Ones, fives, and twenties
Float
Not the big bills
She is supposed to want
She lets them fly around
In disrepair
Crumpled
And half lost

To show she doesn't care
About this stuff
That seems to run
The world
Tells her that
Her treatment of
This paper
Speaks of how
She sees herself

Not having much of it
Has made her feel small
And yet she knows
Wads of paper worth
Do nothing for
Her heart

She struggles with
Its effect on her
She cannot call it
Love or hate
It's more like some
Awful vegetable
You know you should eat
But really dislike

It's survival
That's all
How much does
She really need?

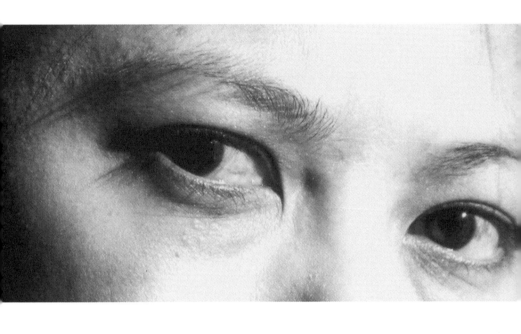

She   29

Is it worth?
Losing herself
Her creativity
Her dreams

Is it worth?
Feeling less
Because someone else
Has more?

When she listens
To her soul
It tells her
What's meaningful is free

The day to day
Simplicities
Of nature
And her dog

Love, family, and friends
Giving back in a
Heartfelt way
Chase away her
Money-hate
Its power over her

Focusing on
Who she is
The only choice
She has

The money
Will come and go
It speaks nothing
Of her worth

"Worth"

What are your feelings about money? Does your self-esteem seem to be tied to how much or how little money you make? Do you feel like a slave to money? Do you have healthy spending practices? Keep a spending log to see where most of your income is going. Can you simplify your life? Do you want to? Make a list of those things you feel are worthwhile, the activities that fuel your soul. How can you integrate what you love with your desire or need to have a good income?

She

Back up from the Mirror

Back up
From the mirror
Don't look so close
You'll find the flaw
You look for
It is there
And will grow

And if it isn't going
To grow
It might
Just sag
And wither

Turn down
The lights
Don't fuss
And the gray
Will cease to flicker

Skin tight
Hair full
How could she believe
That one day
She would see
Her older self
A different face
Appearing

Age
Acceptance of loss
What was
What might not be
Only the spirit knows

Age and wisdom
Will find each other

Put the mirror down

She

WRITING EXERCISE

"Back up from the Mirror"

How do you feel about aging? What are your fears? What do you
look forward to? What older women do you admire? What is it
about them that you respect: personality, career, attitude,
appearance, health, ability to juggle many roles, all of the above,
or something else?

She

What if this was Alright?

(The spelling "alright" is not considered acceptable
standard English according to the dictionary.
But in this poem I use it anyway, and that's alright. -A.R.)

What if this was alright?
This runny nose
This lukewarm tea
The morning's worries
Rushing over me

What if this messy hair
The quiet
The day's plans
Not yet made
Was alright?

What if being
Wrinkled
Crepey and crinkled
Heavier and dimpled
Waify or wimpy
Was alright?

What if being
Successfully single
Happily coupled
Sometimes sad

Lonely
Independent
Joyful
Doubtful

Overwhelmed

Bored

Mad!

Was alright?

What if being
Less than wealthy
Not entirely
Emotionally and physically
Healthy
Was alright?

What would we do?

This is how
We spend our time
Keeping ourselves
In check
Making ourselves
A total wreck

Alright! Alright!
What if it was
What a relief it would be

WRITING EXERCISE

"What if this was Alright?"

Consider this notion of self-acceptance and what it would mean for you. How would your daily thoughts be different?

She   41

Moth

Wings flap and flutter
Lampshade prison
At dawn

Looming sunrise
What future
When all she can do
Is move in circles
Of panicked flight

Too tired to save
Her soul mate moth
Listening to rhythmic suffering
Pain by her bedside

She drifts back to sleep
Indifferent
Not her usual response

Weariness has caught her
Her own frantic dance
Halted by exhaustion

What lies outside the lampshade?
Giant room
Too much freedom

More comfortable
In sheltered dismay
Frustrated safety
Captured in this tiny town

She moves in circles
Reluctant to slip
Outside the edge
Of the familiar
To face her fears

She

Chasing Shade

She shifts the chair
Chasing shade
It eludes her
Sunlight piercing
Glare in her eyes

She wants to sit in
Shade's cool safety
Darkness
A retreat

So much now
Feels too evident
Not in the mood
For seeing
Even in dappled light
What has gone unseen

She cannot smile
In the brightness
She cannot share stories
In the spotlight

She needs shade now
To regroup
To look inward

Her skin
Feels unfamiliar
No temperature
Quite right

She moves the chair
Her back
To the sun
Warmth on her shoulders
A shift in perspective

She sees others now
In the glow
Of compassion and acceptance
She longs to give herself

WRITING EXERCISE

"Moth"

What is the lampshade in your life? What is keeping you from facing your fears?

"Chasing Shade"

Do you avoid facing problems? How do you make decisions and choices in your life? How can you gain perspective to make healthy decisions? Consider writing, talking to friends, meditating, exercising, spending time with nature, reading, or doing something creative.

She

She Is...

She is...
A girlfriend, a wife
The extension of another
She feels this when she is with him
She looks to him
To gauge her feelings
Of who she should be

She watches for approval
Or sneer of disdain
For something she has said or done
Some gesture that is her
She thinks
Although she is not sure
She only knows herself
Alone

Her skin so thin like parchment paper
She wonders if others can see in
And know how much she hurts and loves
How fragile her appearance of competency

How can he not see
That she needs him to hold her
In all her depths
However uncomfortable
She wants him to dive in with her
And experience
Fullness and emptiness
The infinity of her emotions
The minuteness of the things that touch her

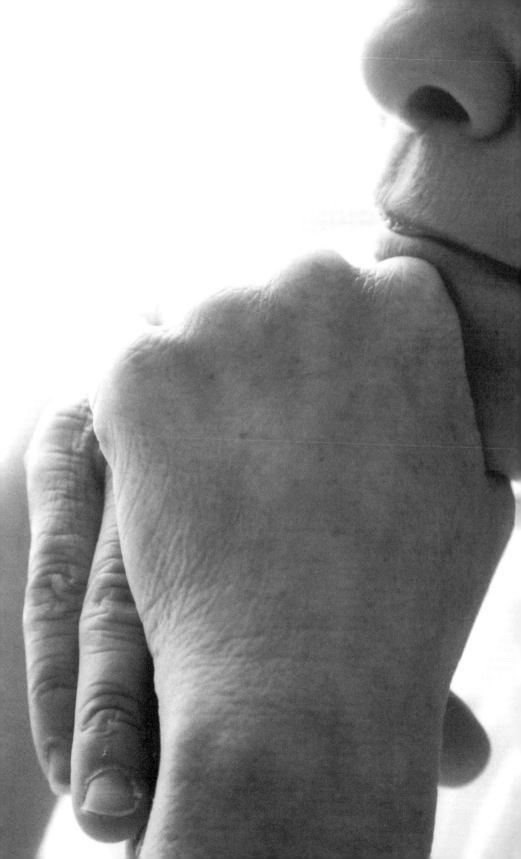

Joy and pain
Wrapped up in her together
In tears
There is laughter
In wit
There are wounds

Does he know this?
Does he wonder about her?
What lies within him
That he will not share?

She thinks she knows him
And yet she doesn't
She wants to know someone
Thoroughly
Predict responses
Create a feeling of safety

Love remains elusive
Slipping away
Whenever she thinks
She has a grip
It changes form

She is a girlfriend, a wife
A woman
She knows only herself
The love and empathy she carries
For all things
The richness of it all

She knows these things
Her own heart
And that is all

"She Is..."

Reflect on this poem. Write about how you can balance a relationship with a healthy sense of self.

She

Where's the Baby?

She dreamt again
Last night
Of the baby
She never had

Her stomach large
Then small
Like a basketball
And then flat

Was it here?
Where has it gone?
Did I lose it somewhere?
Or just forget to have it?

She awakens
Somewhere around three
Anxieties at their peak
She feels her stomach
No baby there
And wonders if she can do it

All her worries
Keeping babies at bay
Some days a relief

Other times
The emptiness prevails
The longing pulls and aches

She can imagine
Waking early
Checking its breathing
Watching it grow

When morning comes
She knows she can do it
It's the night
That tells her no

She

WRITING EXERCISE

"Where's the Baby?"

What times of day do you feel the most anxious? The most
positive? List the fears that might keep you from beginning a
family. If you have a family, what are your concerns about your
children, spouse, or yourself?

She

Complacency

This is it?
Is that all there is?
She wonders
On the couch

The clicker
Changing channels
Too quick
She sits
Lazy and slouched

She looks around
The house
Her home
Her body
Growing old

Lumpy legs
And aching joints
And a boredom
She cannot ignore

She has tried
To blame him
For this blahhhh...
If only this or that
The emptiness
Would fade
Her spark
Rushing back

What is this life?
This day to day to day?
Her expectations
Of growing up

Growing older
The glory
And the fame

And if not these
Then contentment at least
What is it
That she wants?

It is a pit
No activity
No job
No love
Can fill

Her goals
And dreams
Some potential
Not yet seen

She has left them
Somewhere
On the couch
Maybe in
Her routine

It is time
To lift the pillows
Uncover
The dreams

She

WRITING EXERCISE

"Complacency"

Do you feel bored with your life at times? How can you change the patterns in your life that keep you stuck or unmotivated? What steps can you take to spice up your routine?

She

Touch

Touch
Tingles
Her heart

Opens up

Touch
Teaches
Her heart

Opens up

Touch
Transforms
Her heart

Opens up

Touch
Longing
Forward
To be fed

Hungry
For so long
For tenderness
Not felt

Emptiness
Filling

Touch

How simple
How healing

"Touch"

Could you identify with this poem? How do you meet your needs for touch?

The Song

        She arrives at her house at the usual hour, sets her bag
down, and looks around at the clutter of keepsakes and
memories. The house smells of must, a light perfume, and cat—
a strange and comforting aroma that speaks of home. On this
night, the darkness and perpetual rain have affected her deeply.

        Or was it that song, the song she heard on the drive
home? It pulled the longing up from her belly, through her heart,
to her throat as she swallowed back tears that she could not
decipher. Was it the words or the melody that moved her? She was
aware of the instant when the tenderness touched her, like a man
on the dance floor, and for a moment she believed she could feel
his cheek next to hers. Oh, what a feeling, a melting, a comfort
she has not felt for so long that she does not know why her body
remembers. Why does it tease her by bringing that longing to the
surface?

        It will be a long night. No amount of busyness will distract
her from the notion of closeness, so long forgotten. It lies hidden
in some visceral part of her body. She cringes at the sink,
imagining the comfort of arms around her waist, a kiss on her
neck. Had these ever occurred? She tries to remember. She thinks
they might have long ago, but why crave a memory that may or
may not have happened?

        She remembers feeling this lonely when she was married.
She might even have felt the same pull toward imaginary
tenderness. No wonder she was crying. This touch that she craves
will probably always be a fleeting fantasy, a woman's longing for a
depth of sensitivity difficult to find once a relationship settles in.
The touches become sparse and hurried, isolated to the bedroom,
focused on the goal rather than love. It is over, and the loneliness
deepens. She remembers these feelings with her husband and
how she longed to live alone. Now that lustful dance would be
welcome after such a long stretch without. Her skin and muscles
ache to pull tenderness in.

"The Song"

What feelings came up for you as you read about this older woman struggling with loss and loneliness within relationships? In what ways do you identify with her?

She

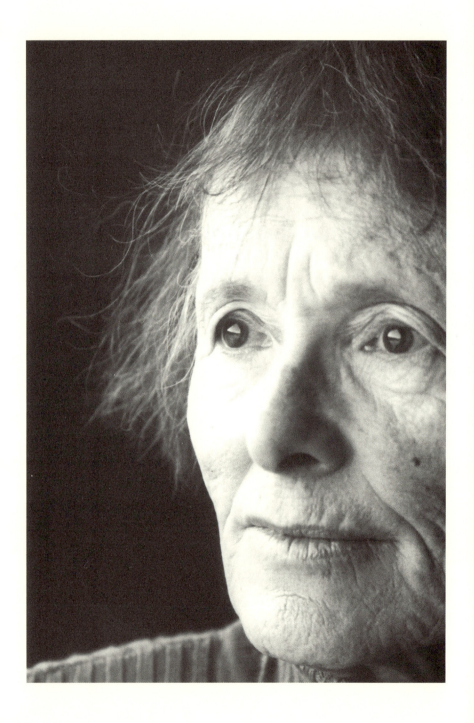

A Wet Spring

Smell of melancholy
Like rain
Not yet realized
Hovering in clouds
The sun overshadowed

Breeze gusts
Familiar air
The sadness of her past
Floods in
With each inhalation

A loneliness
That fits this
Wet spring

Mist longing
A comfort
She recalls
But cannot quite place

Thirsty for love
She so wants
Companionship
To distract her
From these recollections

She

WRITING EXERCISE

"A Wet Spring"

Acknowledge what things trigger feelings of melancholy for you.
How do you take care of yourself when these feelings arise?

She

Two Chairs

She has wandered too far down the beach, lost in heart-shaped rocks, vibrant, glistening stones, sharks' teeth, and petrified wood. She looks up and sees the pavilion and two chairs where she and her father had been sitting, so far off in the distance that she cannot see if he is back yet. He needed to go to the car and would be a while. She anxiously awaits his return as if somehow he could be lost to her on this short journey. He will be lost to her shortly, to the cancer that grows persistently, determined to take him away. So many moments with her father had been lost to her. She always felt them stolen away by the family dysfunction. Somehow it kept getting in the way, as persistent and determined as the cancer. She cannot win either battle, against her irrational family or against the cancer. As she walks toward the chairs she thinks of a line she wrote in a poem long ago, "something lost or never given." She repeats it in her mind over and over.

She ponders her attachment to her father and why it is so powerful; it had always been that way. Maybe it is as simple as understanding one another, a kinship that is rarely found. She is terrified to lose this one. This understanding, her empathy for him, is undeniable and hurts her heart. She cannot save him or her family from disintegrating, a difficult thing for her to accept. She now must focus on keeping herself from breaking down, losing hope, and losing faith. With as much strength as she can muster, she must accept this process as it comes. These thoughts are moving through her mind, backwards and forwards, side to side.

She eventually returns to the chairs, puts a towel down, covers her face with a shirt, and tries to relax. She hears rustling and believes it is him, but it is only a flag in the wind. She wonders if she will look for him, when he is gone, in the familiar gaits and gestures of older men, a voice, a laugh. How does one accept never seeing, talking with, or hugging someone they love ever again?

She almost falls asleep but is roused by something. She looks up and sees that her father has already returned, and is walking away down the beach. She watches him for a moment, imagining him walking farther and farther away until she cannot see him anymore. She almost wants it to happen this way—without the pain of dying. Startled that she is losing precious moments, she leaps up to catch him on his walk, to take his picture, to keep him with her. She hides her tears, knowing it must be hard to die. Who could stand having everyone around them crying? She feigns pleasantness and talks of the beauty of the beach, which seems more potent than she has ever remembered or imagined. They walk to the chairs together, sit for a moment, looking out at the ocean. He says, "This is hard to give up," and she is thinking the same thing.

She

Unfamiliar Darkness

She opens her eyes
To another darkened room
Struggles to orient herself
The door and windows have moved again
Since the night before
Another room in another house
Alone
No familiar breathing
She has become a gypsy
In this last year
In these last months

A traveling caretaker
Her father's cancer
Sent her to her parents' homes
To awaken in various rooms
Listening for his heavy breathing
In the next room

Finally the rollaway bed at Hospice House
Where she continued to listen
For his breathing
Rattling and strained
Until it finally ceased

Now she does not know
How to orient herself
Where to put these feelings of grief
Where to put the love
How to let go of that connection
And move forward

His dying had consumed her
For a year
Her family's sadness had consumed her
For a lifetime

She must say goodbye
To so many parts of herself
Many memories
Many comforts

She hopes to let go of anger
To be reborn
To a more tender place
She hopes to find home

She

"Two Chairs"

Have you faced the prospect of losing someone you love to illness or an accident? What are your fears when you think about losing a parent or loved one? How can you prepare yourself better for such loss? Consider attending a counseling group or share your concerns with friends and family.

"Unfamiliar Darkness"

Have you ever experienced a loss so painful that your life was altered? Reflect on that experience. How did you manage to get through it? Did anything positive emerge from that process? How has the experience changed you?

She

She

Sea Morning

Pristine morning
Has found her
On this bench

Bikes reel past
Tiny bridge
Inviting back fishermen
Passers-by talk quietly
Honoring morning's grace

Summer sea air
A perfume she would wear
Bottle and keep
Memories

Childhood vacations
Bike rides with dad
The boardwalk
At dawn

Friendly strangers
Part of some
Secret cluster
Of those who understand
Its treasure

Adolescence
The Jersey Shore
With friends
Summer cottages
Sleepy mornings
Sand on barefoot toes
Laughing

Twenties
Cape Cod
Waking outside
Dumpy porch
Honeysuckle heaven

Scrambling through tip jars
For breakfast cash
With friends
Always
Laughing

Early thirties
She lost
The morning
Along with herself

Now
On this bench
Rediscovering
A greater force
She once knew
As a child

Boardwalk dawn by
The shore

She

WRITING EXERCISE

"Sea Morning"

Consider the decades of your life and what memories are the most powerful and meaningful. How have you changed? How have you remained the same?

She

Two Chairs Wait

Two chairs wait
For a tender older couple
Walking hand in hand
Taking in the peacefulness of age
Noticing every flicker of light
Every seagull
Every egret
The joy of being truly connected

Two chairs wait
For an estranged couple
Walking in a pair
The distance apparent between them
Resistant to the healing power of nature
Noticing their own resentment
Aging bodies
Lost dreams
The thoughts that reel continually
In their separate minds

Two chairs wait
For a young mother and her son
Collecting seashells and sharks' teeth
Stooping down with each spotted treasure
Noticing the warmth and ease of vacation
The uninterrupted special moments together

Two chairs wait
For a dying father and his daughter
Walking in slower labored steps
The daughter awkward
Trying to gauge his gait
Noticing the stunning beauty of this beach
The warmth and sparkling brilliance of the water
The frailty and preciousness of all things

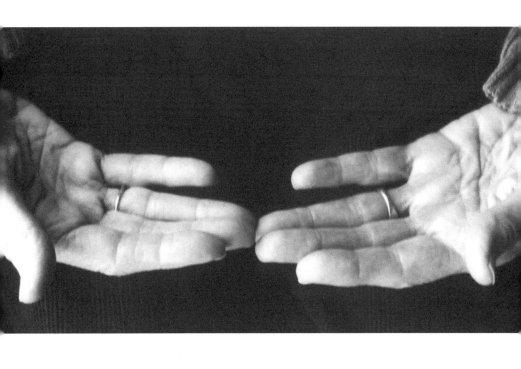

She

"Two Chairs Wait"

Read each stanza of the poem again. Which relationship dynamic moved you and how? Begin writing about the poignant moments in your life.

She

The Light

His space is dark
So dim the light
"I'm over here" she says
He staggers to the right

"Over here" she says
He walks toward her
Groping
Losing his way
His darkness follows
Consuming and gray

Hope and love
Obstacles in his path
He trips
Crushes her heart

Lost
He's angry and powerless now
Guide him
Guide her
Please show them how

Her love so tender
Stepped on again
Broken pieces
She sweeps them up

Relentless hope
Determination
Too futile for mending

Love turns to dust
Her light grows dim
Brightness awaits her
Far from him

She 91

WRITING EXERCISE

"The Light"

What does "the light" represent for you? Are there people in your life that dim your light? How do you feel about these relationships? How can they be improved?

She

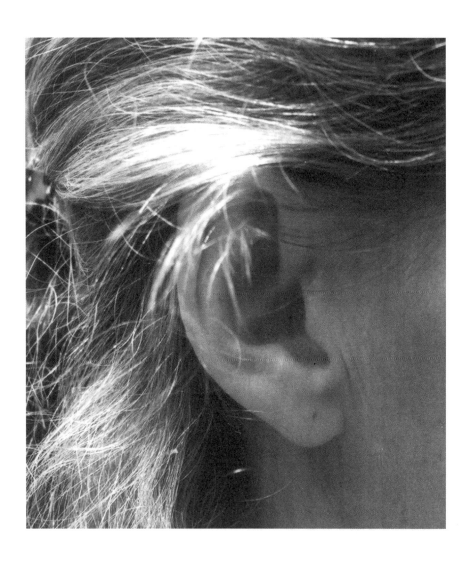

What She Craved

The silence
Of loneliness
Allows her to hear
Traffic on distant streets
The rhythmic hum
Of appliances

Faint breaths
Of her dog
Her own breathing
Her own heart
Beating

Sensations heightened
Her emotions raw
She feels the walls
Closing in

Her world
Grows smaller
She had imagined it
Blossoming with change
Is this the feeling of freedom?

She

The quiet
She craved
Now sounds
Too loud

Her past self
The deadened version
Seems alluring now

This loneliness
Is something
To contend with

Far more intense
Than any man
She faces herself

"What She Craved"

What does it mean to face yourself? What do you realize about yourself when you spend time alone? Write about the difference between loneliness and solitude.

She

Is She Somebody?

Is she somebody?
Eyes look away
Who is she
Without his gaze?

Her heart
Imagines stopping
Last breaths taken in
Is she somebody?
Without him

Is she somebody?
The days she sits around
Or goes to work
Relationship not found
Without him
No ground

A single woman
Not seen
A missing woman
Without her man

Keep looking
You might be bound
To loneliness

A new belief
To heal her heart
Maybe not lost at all
But found

Who are you?

WRITING EXERCISE

"Is She Somebody?"

Have you ever identified with these feelings of loss living without a partner? What does the last stanza mean for you, what is it to be "found"?

She

She

The Gaze

Searching for the gaze
In faces
Staring back

The imagined look
That says, "I love you"
Full of acceptance
Of all she is
And tries to be

It sees
Her heart
It does not waver
It does not flee

Gaze's loss
Has traveled with her
Into adulthood
And she wants its love
For her child

The little girl within
That lived
Too long without
That love
She yearns to see
In pupils
Staring back

She is a woman
Learning
It is time
To give the gaze
And let go
This feeling of lack

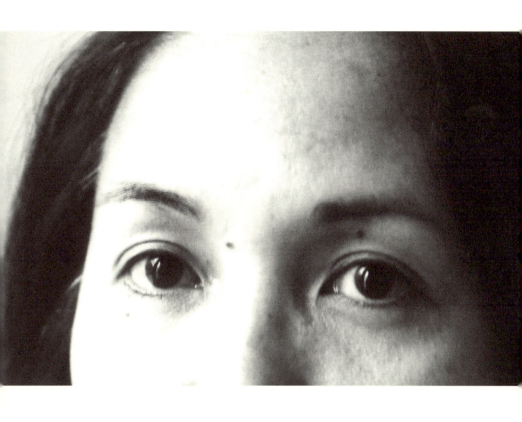

She

"The Gaze"

Where do you search for the gaze? Who do you give your gaze to? Notice the feelings that arise as you give and receive the gaze.

She

Home

She sits
And contemplates
Friends' sanctuaries
Comforted by
Keepsakes and music
Memories
Not her own

Heart rocks
Line windows
Grace and hope
Appear in books
On walls
Words of inspiration
Fill emptiness
Of love's loss

Their houses
An affirmation
Of selves relying on selves
Sacred spaces
Of healing
Shared with the unfortunate

Tears well
Gratefulness fills
Her heart
At the comfort
Of a home
Of women
On their own

Her car and dog
The love of friends
Her only constants

Her home
Resides somewhere
Within
It must
Be carried like a sign
From dwelling
To dwelling

No longer
A house shared
With a man
That home filled
With strife
Torn down

Now
On a journey
Taking her
Away from the life
Imagined

She has renamed
Home
And builds it
Out of self

She

WRITING EXERCISE

"Home"

Home means different things for different people. Describe what a healthy and fulfilling home life would mean for you. Where is home for you?

She

Winter Gathering

This air is cool
The tea is hot
Friends gather
in a booth

The conversation
Moves
Head and eyes
Switch direction
Interests shift
Sensibilities astute

Absorbed
Distracted
Wisdom
Humor
And pain

Each week
Next to and across
Faces and bodies change
The conversation
Remains the same

She

The longing for love
Careers, family, and friends
The balance of all
And the absence of some

They discuss
Like a team
The best approach
For living

Time moves
Quickly
The clock
Interrupts
Laughter and connection
They say goodbye with hugs
Moving on to their day

WRITING EXERCISE

"Winter Gathering"

Gather together a group of women friends; try to meet every week or every month. Meet at restaurants, coffee shops, people's houses. Keep the venue the same or change it. Talk, laugh, and enjoy each other's company.

The Story

She put her book down
Eyes welling up
One character
Truly touched her heart

She felt like this woman
As a little girl
With tears that came
Too quickly
And lasted much
Too long

It was empathy
A quality to admire
But hers
Was much too strong

To notice
Every bug and creature
All their pain
And loneliness
An overwhelming burden

Did she really feel
The truth?
That hurt and loss abound

Sometime later
She grew up
And realized
There are gifts that come
With a tender heart

A unifying notion
That she is not alone
Pleasure and grief
Are present for all
So why stay in all that sorrow?

It's clearer now
It's time to stop
Hiding out and
Playing small

A confusing time
Of self-discovery
Not always liking
What she finds

Within
And in the world
There is certainly
Not perfection

But on more days now
Life shines with possibilities
Not the dismal and the dark
But a thrilling awareness
Of each moment
Her empathy has grown kind

WRITING EXERCISE

"The Story"

How are you involved in your community? Would you like to become more involved? What group or organization do you believe could use your help? Perhaps you are already involved and feel that there is no time left for yourself. How can you balance self-care and care for others?

She

Grace

Grace
A woman of great tenderness
And wisdom
She waits for grief
And teaches us lessons

Lovely and bright
She beckons from afar
Invite her
Closed hearts must
Be left ajar

She enters there
The source
We all share

She grows like ivy
On dwellings of bitterness
Caverns of coldness
Fill with warmth
She wraps the wounded
In blankets of love

Grace
Once only a guest
Now friend
Her dignity and strength
Teach us how to mend

"Grace"

What does the word "Grace" mean to you? If Grace were a friend, what painful experiences would you share with her? How could she help you to heal?

She

The Alchemist

The alchemist
Attempts to change
Base metals into gold

The word emerged one day
As she reflected
On her goals

Her motivations
From childhood until now
Turning pain into joy
She thought she could do it somehow

Remaining attentive
Quiet and strong
Keeping things light with her humor
Expressing empathy and love

So consumed with her goal
Of curing others' pain
She forgot to tend her own
Perplexed by her own sadness
Not clear about its source

The alchemist
Has good intentions
The dictionary says
Searching for the universal solvent
The elixir of life
A magical cure

The alchemist
Was he ever successful?
History tells us
No
Her attempts equally futile

The alchemist would have done better
To see himself instead
To ponder his motivations
For fixing and changing matter
Why not just leave it alone
What's so wrong with a base metal?

Fixing and changing others
Wears a person down
She sees this now
To let it go
Is the only magic

The only thing she can change
The person within herself
A simple notion
Yet hard to embrace
She is putting her potions down

WRITING EXERCISE

"The Alchemist"

Women are often viewed as caretakers. Consider your motivations when you take care of others. Think about your desire to control. Are you trying to change others? How can you focus on your own self-growth and health?

She

How About

Her fears are based
On assumptions
On notions of being
One more expendable woman

To a man
With only
His own goals and agendas
He drives
And she cannot
Touch the wheel
Without the fear of loss

She cannot bear
One more
Unfinished romance
One more
Beginning and ending

She wants to
Share the journey
In friendship and respect
Without notions
Of power over
And the underpowered

Who is in control?
Why not meet
On common ground
On even soil
Without hills and trenches
Without the dance
Of near and far

How about close
With room to breathe
How about space
With the comfort of
Companionship

These are notions
She would rather ponder
These are assumptions
She would like to find true

She

Dare She Say?

Wonder what he's thinking
What lies beneath
Friendliness and concern
Does he want to
Know her
Or just take and hurt?

The eyes are clear
They seem true
No trust
Her instincts have
Misguided her

Confronted with kindness
Will she love again?

Dare she say
Dare she say
"I see goodness and a heart"
Imagined ?
She wants to know

Her heart
A day lily
Opens and closes
In rhythms
Of trust
And mistrust

"How About"

Focus on stanzas five and six. Does this idea represent a healthy relationship for you? What are your expectations of a relationship?

"Dare She Say?"

Do you have trust issues stemming from past relationships? What can you do to start to rebuild a sense of trust within relationships?

She

Not Enough

Not enough
She thought
Not pretty enough, smart, creative, funny, thin, exciting, rich,
outgoing, reserved, ambitious, athletic, young, healthy, focused,
giving, mothering, patient, or loving enough...

Her list was long
She was proud of it
Yet she knew it wasn't complete
So many "not enoughs" to add
If she could only think harder
Her list grew large
As the space left for
Possibilities, potential, and hope dwindled

She awoke one day
Her body immobile
Her vision blurred with tears
Her ears filled with "not enough"
Her mouth parched with negativity

It was on this morning
Her life opened up
She could not do "not enough" any longer
She mumbled "I'm enough today"
Over and over

Her limbs loosened
Her eyes widened
The birds began to call

She stood up
And "not enough"
Slid away
Like droplets on the floor

"I'm enough"
Felt light and easy
She smiled broadly
And began wondering
With love
About others and the world

She

WRITING EXERCISE

"Not Enough"

What does your "not enough" list include? Write it down. Is it long or brief? Try saying "I'm enough" to yourself each day whenever negative self thoughts come up. Notice the difference in the way you begin to feel about yourself. Heighten your awareness of how many times you say some version of "not enough" to yourself.

She

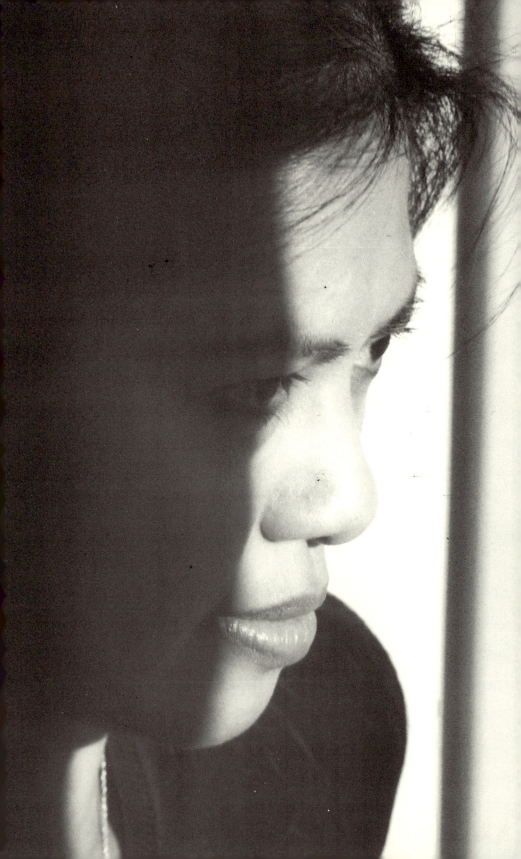

Ordinary to Extraordinary

The kitchen is bright
Leaf shadows
On the pantry door
Edges crisp and dark
Sun emerging

Wicker chairs
Illuminated
Patterned details
Revealed

To wake up
To the extraordinary
Is powerful

Days become
Ripe, full, and sweet
Like the pear
At breakfast

Notice
The trickle
Of water

Down pipes
Toward the kitchen

The hum
Of heat
Pushing through grates
Throughout the house

One could
Wait for these
Moments
All day

Or seek them
Washing the dishes
Walking the dog
At a desk
In the car

Alone
Or with others
Life appears

She

Woods Walk

Dusk light
Low
Warm and orange
Trickles through trees
Hurried gusts
Of day
Cease

Only breeze
Soft
A gentle ending
Revisited
Again and again

Tomorrow
She will find
Comfort
In woods
Like in a friend

"Ordinary to Extraordinary"

Try this exercise: Take 15 to 30 minutes to become fully aware of your senses and your surroundings. Take three deep breaths to relax and focus. This can be anywhere or any time. Write down your observations. What moments really stood out for you? Try this exercise daily.

"Woods Walk"

Consider what places bring you a feeling of comfort and well-being. Make a list and try to visit one of these places at least once a week.

She

Her Dog

Her dog
Just under foot
Constant and true
His fur a familiar cushion
Moves

Glancing over
From across the room
Toward her
A constant vigil
Of love

Takes many forms
This is one
She cannot repress
He's always there
Waiting to express
Loyalty

In every gesture
Enthusiasm
For her
For life
He teaches her
Lessons
Not awakened before

It's been here
All along
In his breath
His fur
Loving connection
Awaits her

In forms
Beyond a man
In the trees
The birds
The land

Offer love
It comes back to him
Her dog
Lying calmly
Take it in

"Her Dog"

Do you have a pet, child, someone or something that represents unconditional love in your life? Write about that experience.

Write about why it might be difficult for you to be vulnerable with another person. What are the fears that come up in intimate relationships?

Broken

Is she broken?
She's not sure
So much taken
Shaken to the core

Pieces scatter
Sharp shards
Are few
Resentment and fear
Form a tiny pile

The softer pieces
More plentiful
Blurred edges
Much nicer to pick up

In them
She finds
Many hues
Green, purple, red, and blue

Love and kindness
Humor
Joy
Creativity
And passion

They were there
All along
It took her bottle breaking
Her life a scattered mess

It took
Being broken
To find the pieces
Hidden for so long
Within some darkened vessel
That was not hers at all

Grateful now
For pain and upheaval
Those colorful gems
Now hers

She watches them
As a new
And beautiful vessel
Takes form

She

Desire

Tendrils reaching
Passion is red
Pulled in directions
Upward
Wanting to shed
The past

Future
Unknown
Desire
To be fed

Love

Arrives
In a form
Not outside
It is toward
Her own heart
She is being led

She

"Broken"

Reflect upon the lessons you have learned through painful experiences and how you have grown. What are the inner positives from which you can create a new vessel, new perspective, and new life?

She

"Desire"

Write your own desire poem.

She

Let It Change You

When you lose things
So close to your heart
You cannot imagine the emptiness
Let it change you

When you wonder
When the hurt will cease
When the tears will pass
When the numbness
Will break open into life again
Let it change you

When life seems
More unfair than fair
When injustice seems to reign
And contaminates your thoughts
Let it change you

In the moments
Between darkness and darkness
When the heat of the sun
Shadow of a leaf
Gentle cooing of a dove
Beckon you to notice
Let it change you

When eyes seem to see inside you
And find the hurt
When you cannot help but smile
At the kindnesses
Let it change you

When laughter
Appears out of nowhere
When moments feel
Poignant and lovely
Let it change you

When your heart reopens
After having shut down for a while
And all that remains
Is the love
Let it change you

She

"Let It Change You"

Write about what the phrase "Let it change you" means for you. When times are difficult, consider focusing on acceptance. Allow yourself to feel all levels of emotions during painful experiences. Try not to judge yourself but rather acknowledge the thoughts and feelings as just thoughts and feelings. You can write about them or share them with others. Notice how your feelings change and evolve.

She

About the Author

Amy Rowling is a teacher, photographer, and writer living in Knoxville, Tennessee. She has a Master of Fine Arts degree, with a concentration in photography, and a Bachelor of Fine Arts, with art teaching certification. She spent twelve years living, teaching, and developing her creative talents in Cape Cod, Massachusetts. At present, she is the education and prevention coordinator of a sexual assault crisis center in Knoxville, developing and teaching prevention programs for children, adolescents, and adults throughout the community. She is also sharing this book, *She*, with groups of women as they work on their personal growth and self-actualization.

She

To order this book or
other books published
by

Word Studio

please visit
www.word-studio.com
or call
520-320-0758